Garfield Treasury

Garfield Treasury

BY: JIM DAVIS

BALLANTINE BOOKS • NEW YORK

The Sunday strips appearing here in color were previously included in black and white in GARFIELD At Large, GARFIELD Gains Weight, GARFIELD Bigger Than Life, and GARFIELD Weighs In.

Library of Congress Catalog Card Number: 82-90221

ISBN: 0-345-30713-5

First Edition: November 1982

Cover design by Brian Strater and Neil Altekruse

Designed by Gene Siegel

10   9   8   7

7/23

BEWARE OF CAT!

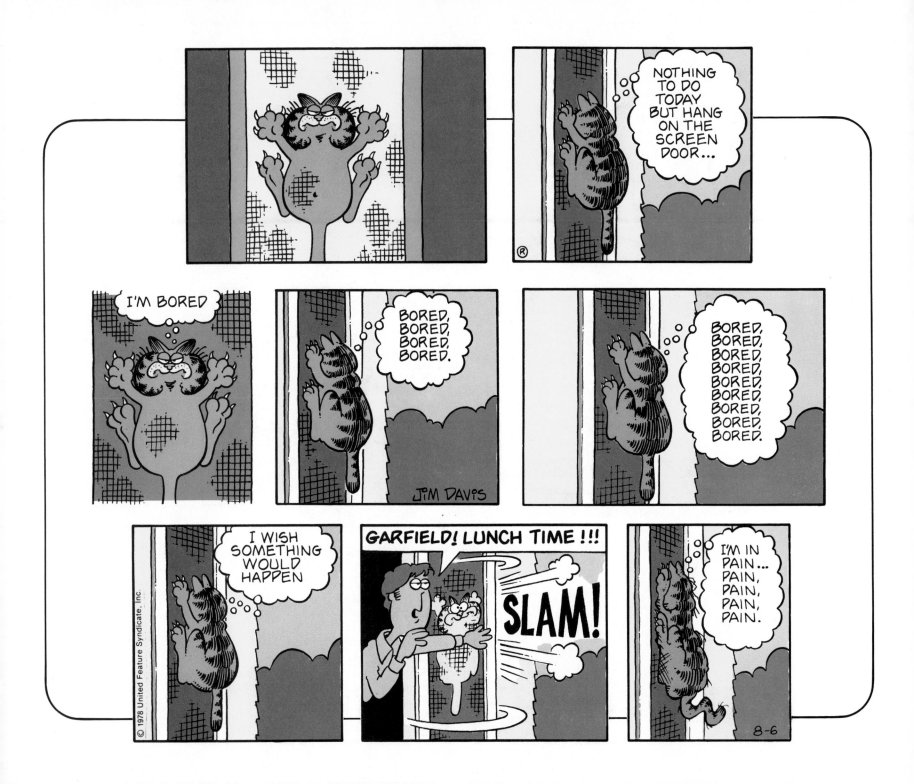

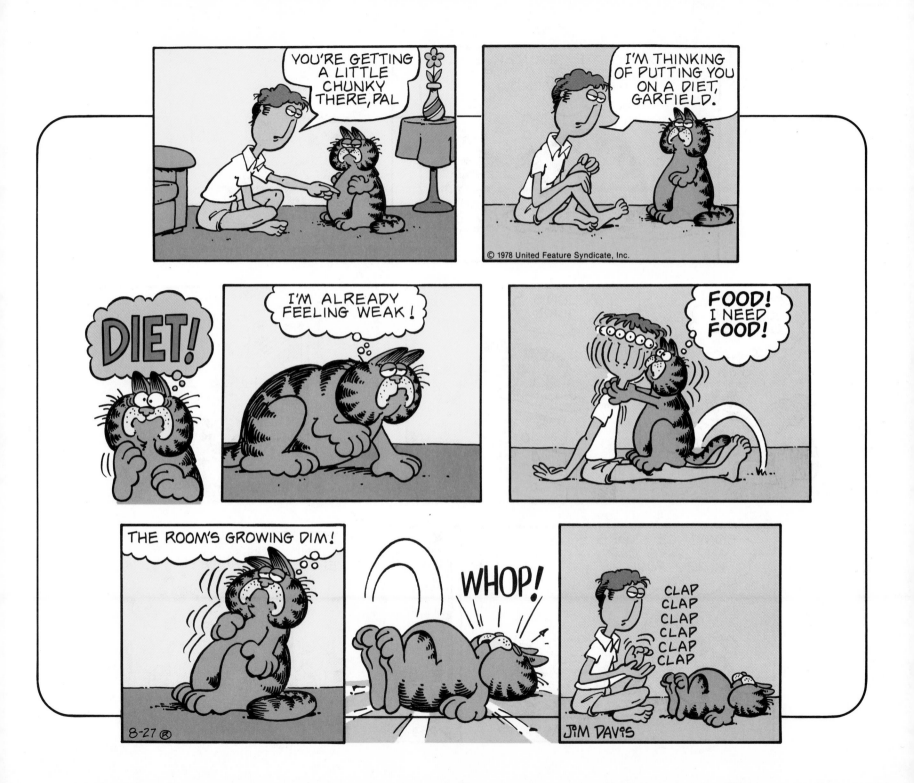

JIM DAVIS

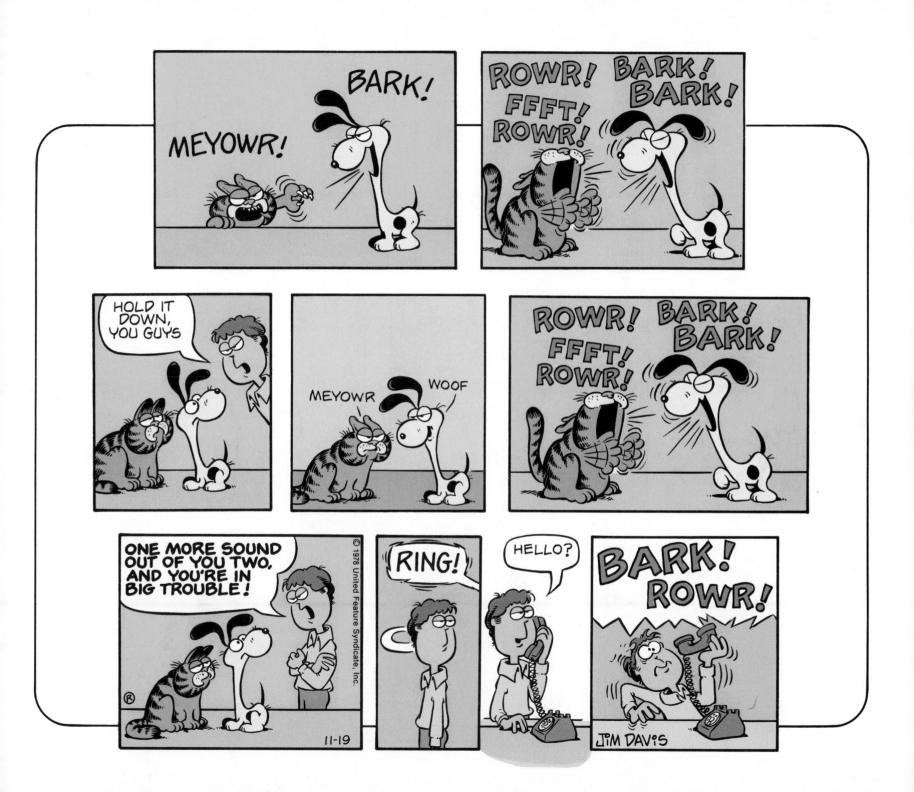

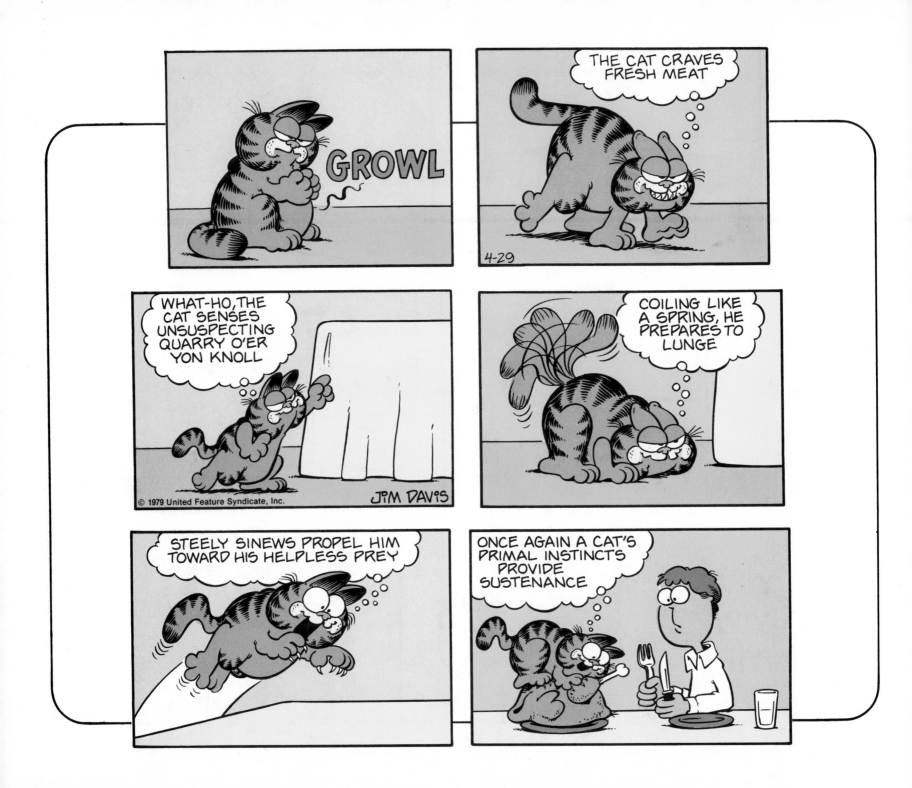

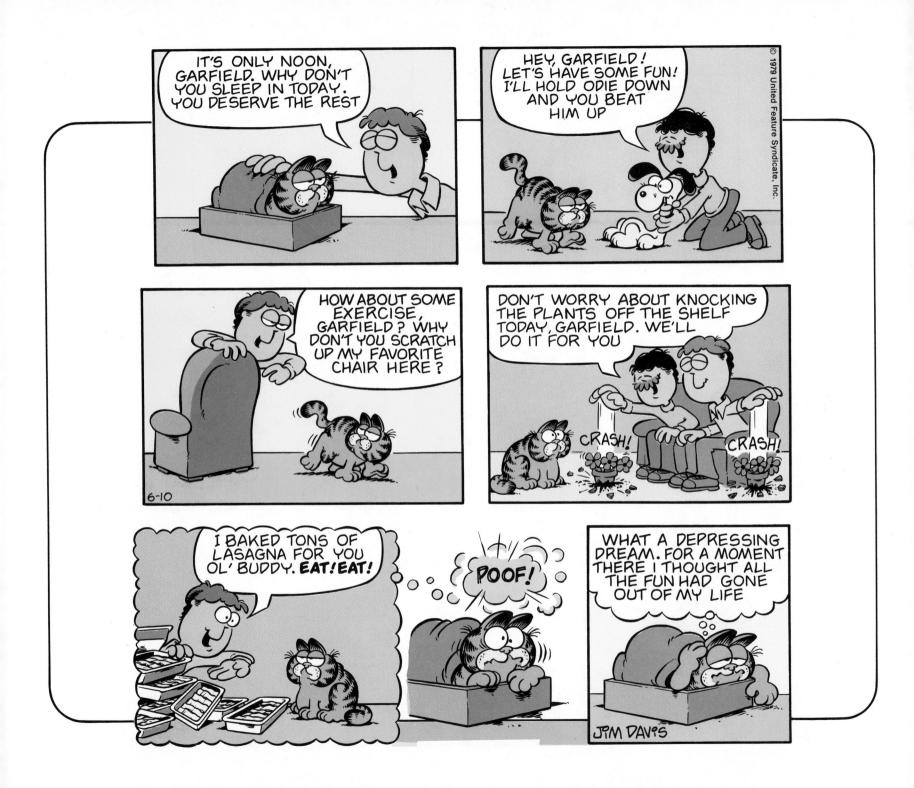

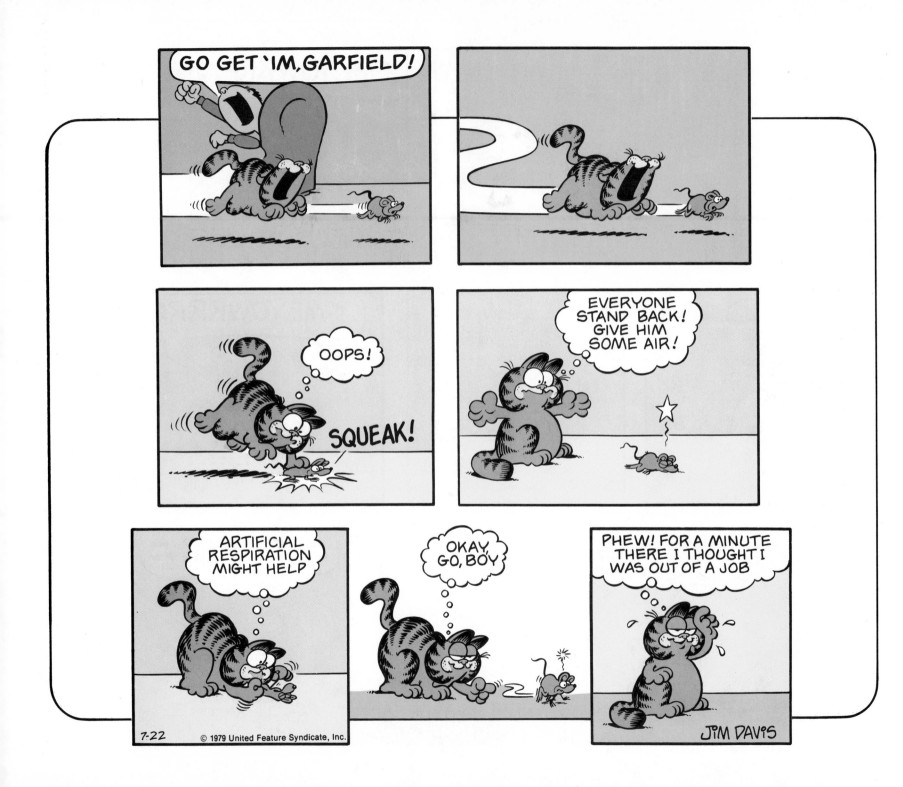

© 1980 United Feature Syndicate, Inc.

JIM DAVIS

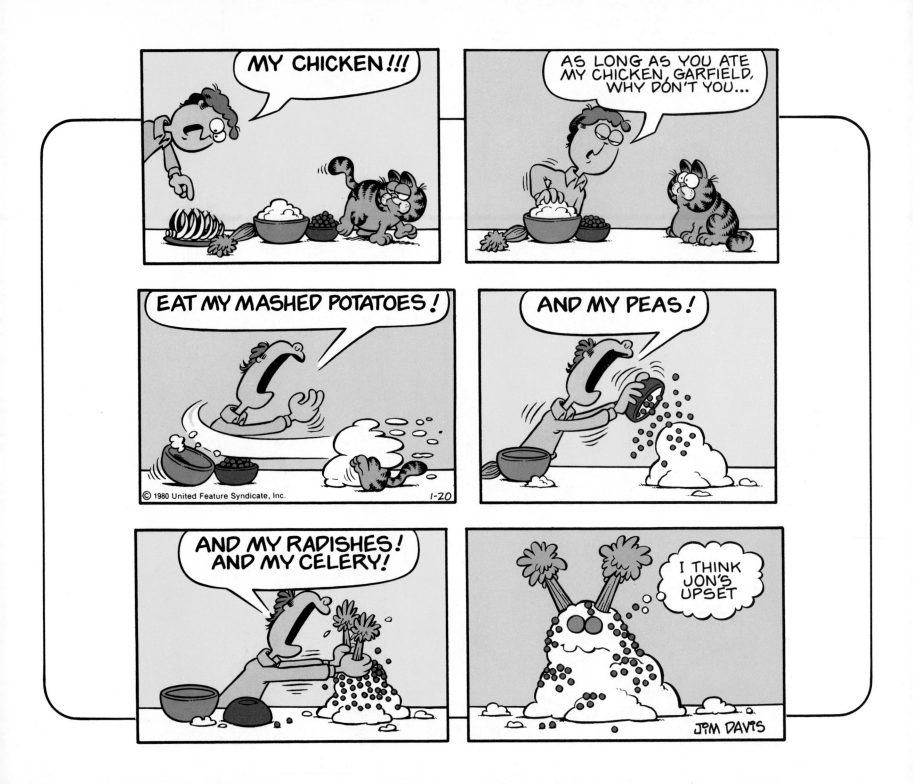

2-17   JiM DAViS

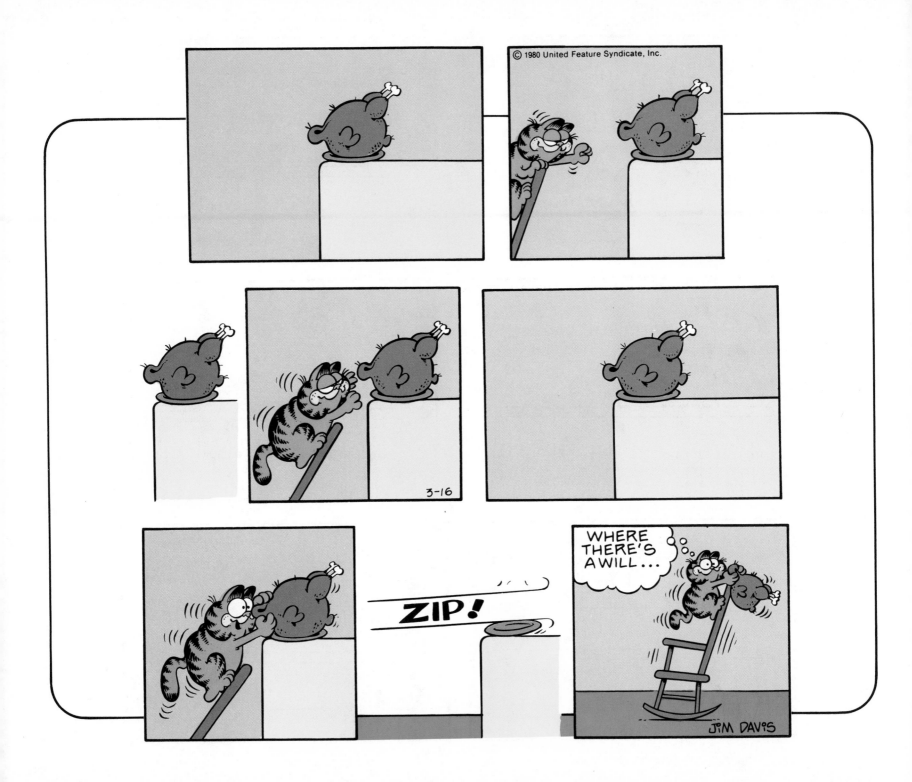

6-22

JIM DAVIS

© 1980 United Feature Syndicate, Inc.

About Jim Davis

Jim Davis was born July 28, 1945, in Marion, Indiana. After growing up on a farm near Fairmount, Indiana, with about 25 cats, Jim attended Ball State University in Muncie. As an Art and Business major he distinguished himself by earning one of the lowest accumulative grade point averages in the history of the university.

During the two-year stint at a local advertising agency Jim met and married wife Carolyn, a gifted singer and elementary school teacher.

In 1969 he became the assistant to Tom Ryan on the syndicated comic strip, TUMBLEWEEDS. In addition to cartooning, Jim maintained a career as a freelance commercial artist, copywriter, and radio-talent and political campaign promoter.

His hobbies include chess, sandwiches, and good friends. A new pastime is playing with his son, James Alexander.

In 1978 United Feature Syndicate gave the nod to GARFIELD.

Jim explains, "GARFIELD is strictly an entertainment strip built around the strong personality of a fat, lazy, cynical cat. It's the funniest strip I've ever seen. GARFIELD consciously avoids any social or political comment. My grasp of the world situation isn't that firm anyway. For years, I thought OPEC was a denture adhesive."

The strip is pumped out daily, in a cheerful atmosphere among friends. Valette Hildebrand is assistant cartoonist; artists include Kevin Campbell, Neil Altekruse, Mike Fentz, Brian Lum, and Dave Kuhn; Ron Tuthill is production manager; Jill Hahn is office manager; Dick Hamilton is business manager; Larry Carmichael is pilot for the group's corporate plane; and Julie Hamilton is president of Paws, Incorporated, the company that handles the merchandising of the characters in the strip.

"To what do I attribute my cartooning ability?" Jim asks. "As a child I was asthmatic. I was stuck indoors with little more than my imagination and paper and pencil to play with. While asthma worked for me, I wouldn't recommend it for everyone.

"Do I like cartooning?....It's nice work if you can get it."